Songs from the Earth

The voice from magical plants
Oracle Book

Distributed in Global : yokowee.com
Distributed in Japan : ruan.y.s.p@aol.jp , http://ameblo.jp/ruan-work/

Scans of the Mandala Art to digital format by: artistisland.com
Printed by Creatspace.com

ISBN 978-0615705668

Thanks to everyone who discovered this book from the many possibilities out there.

Yoko Y. Wee

Index

How to use the Book
How to use the Aroma Oils
Prologue

How to use this book?

1. Either ask your question or
without a question (with your empty mind)
before opening the book.

2. Open the book and choose the Mandala that you are most interested in.
You will find the message that you need.

There is no coincidence, just necessity....

3. You may also use this book for daily, weekly, or
monthly topics to develop yourself.

How to use the Aroma oils?

To inhale

1. Put 3-5 drops of Aroma oil into a diffuser for your room.

2. Put 3-5 drops of Aroma Oil with hot water into a bowl or a cup.

   Always put the hot water into the bowl or cup first, then add the oils. You can put it on your desk at work or beside your bed to inhale the scent, anywhere you wish to enjoy the fragrance .   ! Caution: please keep out of reach of children and pets.

Personal spray

Put 5-10 drops of the Aroma Oil with 2 oz of distilled Water and Witch Hazel alcohol (1/2 tsp /2.5ml) into a glass sprayer. Please try to use a light blocking bottle like green or blue. (Dilution for under 1% for this recipe) Always put water in the spray bottle first, then alcohol, then the Aroma Oils. Shake well. Spray around your Aura whenever you feel it is needed.

Recipe for your relaxing bath time

Choose one of these recipes and put into your hot bath.

! Some oils are strong and may irritate your skin. Please be cautious of any allergy from the recipes. If you are concerned about a reaction, please see a doctor immediately.

1. 3-5 drops of Aroma oils with honey (1tbsp) and a cup of milk (or soy milk)

2. 3-5 drops of Aroma oils with 2 oz of sea salt, and 2 oz of baking soda

3. 3-5 drops with 4 oz of Japanese Sake.

....

! This book is only for inhaling use only (except for the bath recipes) to assist you in meditation, develop your emotions and for chakra healing. If you want to use for your skin or internally, or other uses, please consult a professional. If you are pregnant, nursing, under medication or under 7 years old, please consult a professional before use as well.

Prologue

There are messages always singing
through the plants around us.

We just need to listen
and look carefully.

They are always there for us....

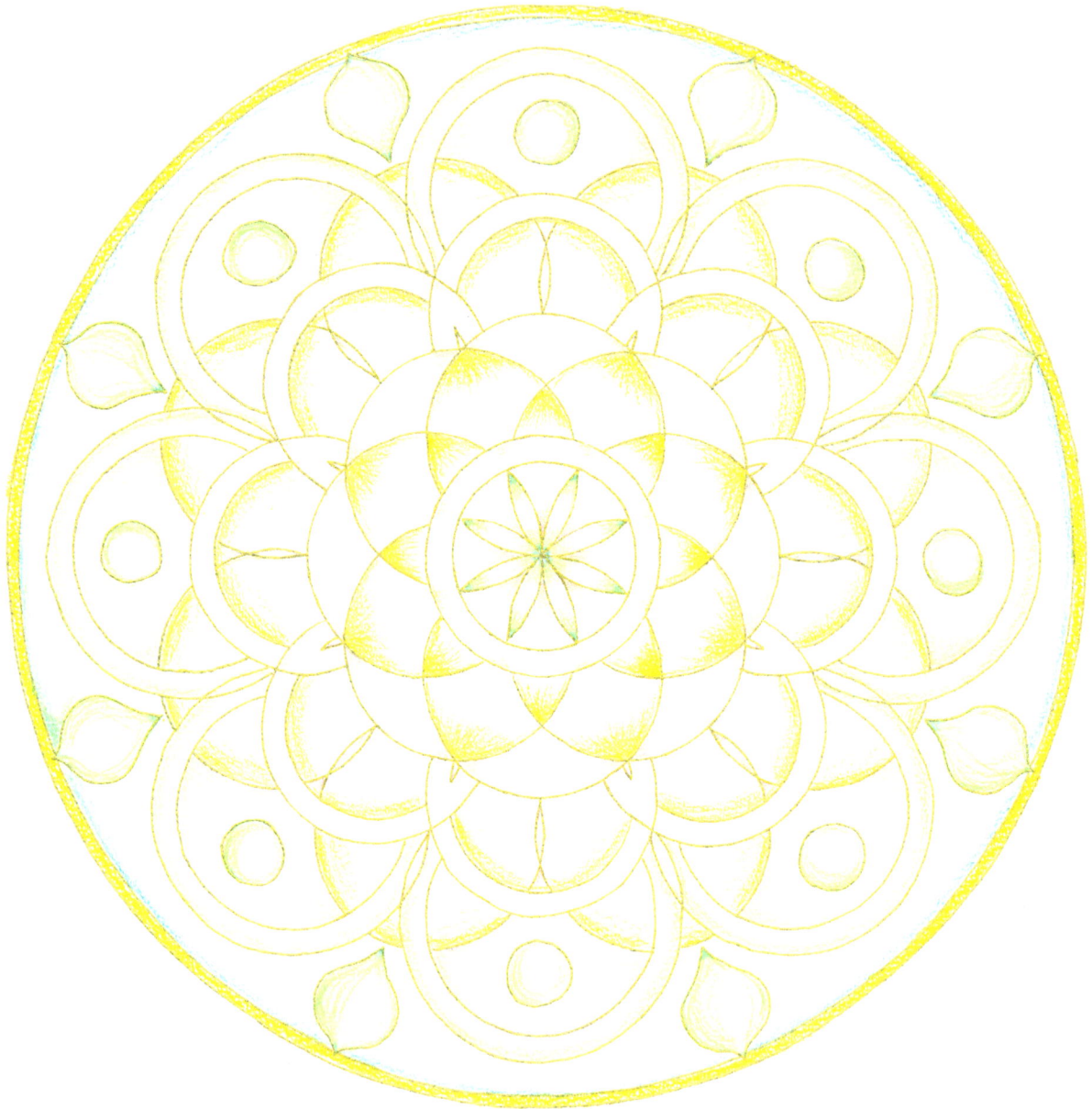

Atmosphere of kindness.

Try to remember the pure spirit you embodied when you were a child.
You knew that Nature was always with you, hugging and giving you
unconditional love since the day you were born. That Love is very warm and
will always watch over you. Please know that you are not alone.
Please, look up. Please, feel alive.
Realize that not only the things you can see give you love
but also things you can't see.
You are wearing this atmosphere like a veil.

Neroli

Neroli relieves all your stress and will give you a blanket of warm and kind
energy that your soul needs.

Just Be Yourself.

Being too critical of yourself will destroy your body.
If you set an image of yourself too high, you will never be happy with whom you are. You are supposed to have experiences along the way but being critical can block you from having these experiences.
You will be unhappy and undernourished.
Find the courage to reset yourself and just be who you are.
This will give you the truest happiness in you life.

Grapefruit

Grapefruit scent helps you rebalance the body and recover from a state of frustration and self-criticism. It will guide you to see reality and set a perfect goal.

Day 3

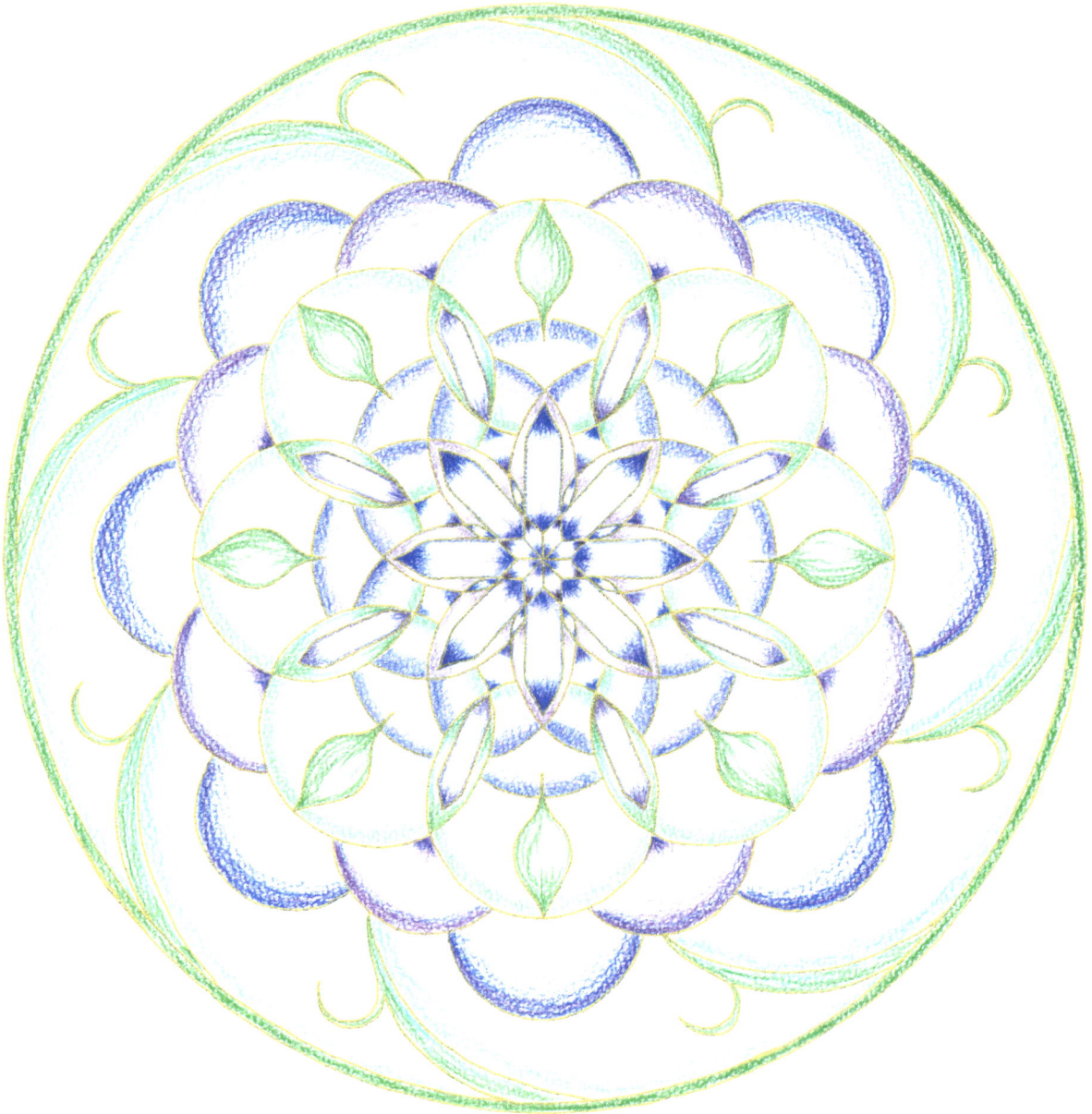

Think with your brain and feel with your heart.

Do not confuse what you feel compared to what you think.
Right now, you are most likely doing too many things that you don't have to do. This will distract you from your goals. You may have lost sight of your goals or have become confused about your path in life, which brings about a sense of frustration. You continue down this path because your brain tells you that you should, but the brain is for thinking, not feeling. Do not let your brain control you, remember, you are living in your heart. So, follow your heart, not your brain. Then you will see that your tree is bushy and grows slowly. Sometimes your tree needs trimming to trigger growth. Then you will see your tree grow huge and even bear fruit. So, even though we usually think with our brain, don't forget it is more important to feel with your heart.

Peppermint

Peppermint scent can have both a warming and cooling effect. It will calm your nerves and open your heart. It will release fear and channel that energy to your heart. It gives you Yin Yang balance.

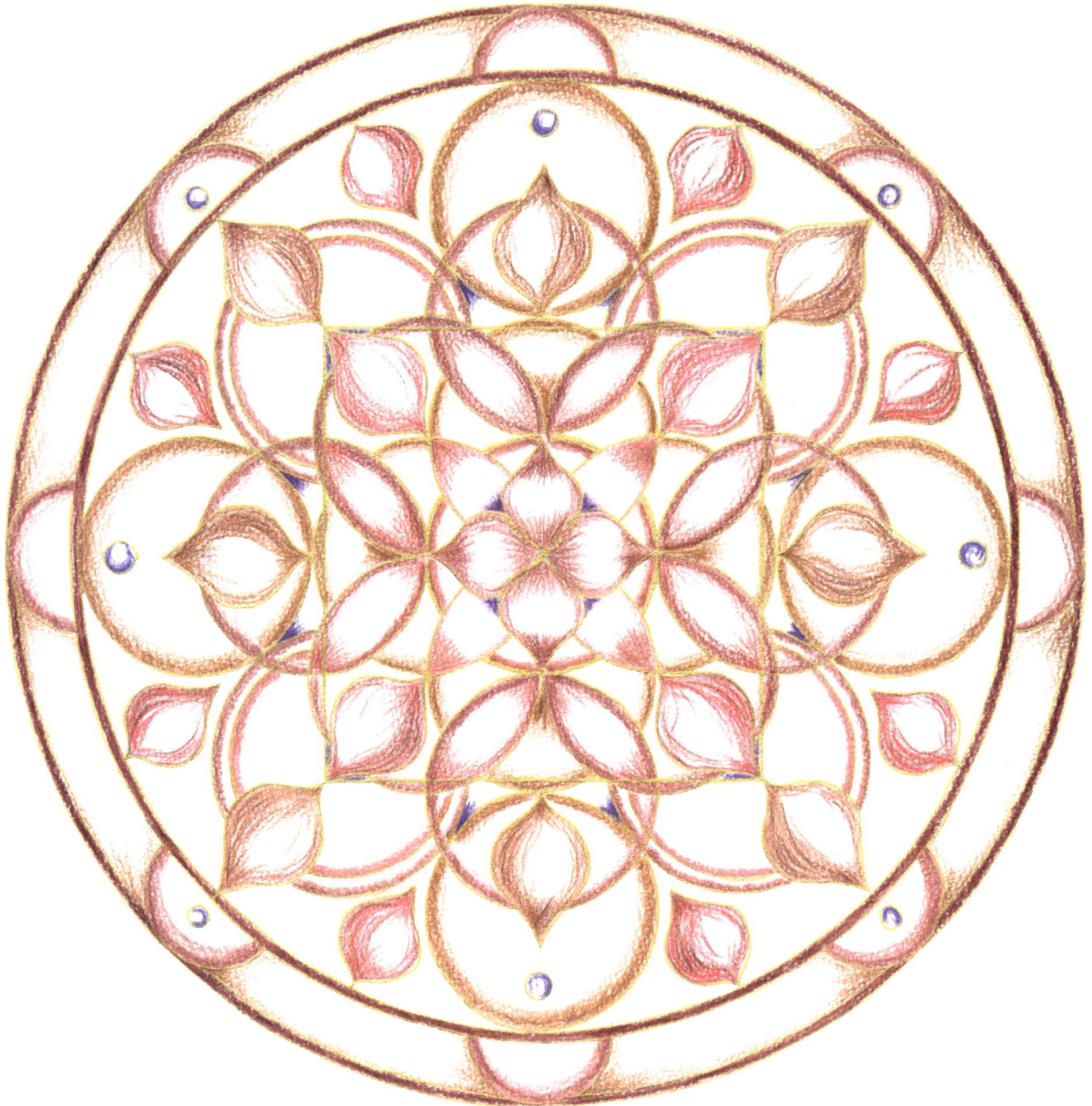

Present Time

Do not ignore things that are happening right now. Everything that happens has meaning. If you put the present aside, you will find it difficult to obtain your goals. The most important thing is not to live in the past and not to worry about the future. Develop yourself from this experience. Think about what you can learn, how to move on from your past and how to live in the present. The Past creates the Present, the Present creates the Future. Please realize you are living in the present time. That is why the gift of living in the now is called "The Present".

Patchouli

Patchouli scent is like the earth and will help in grounding you. It guides you to focus on the present and release your negative feelings about the Past and the Future. It resets you to a good vibration that will keep you focused on the present.

Day 5

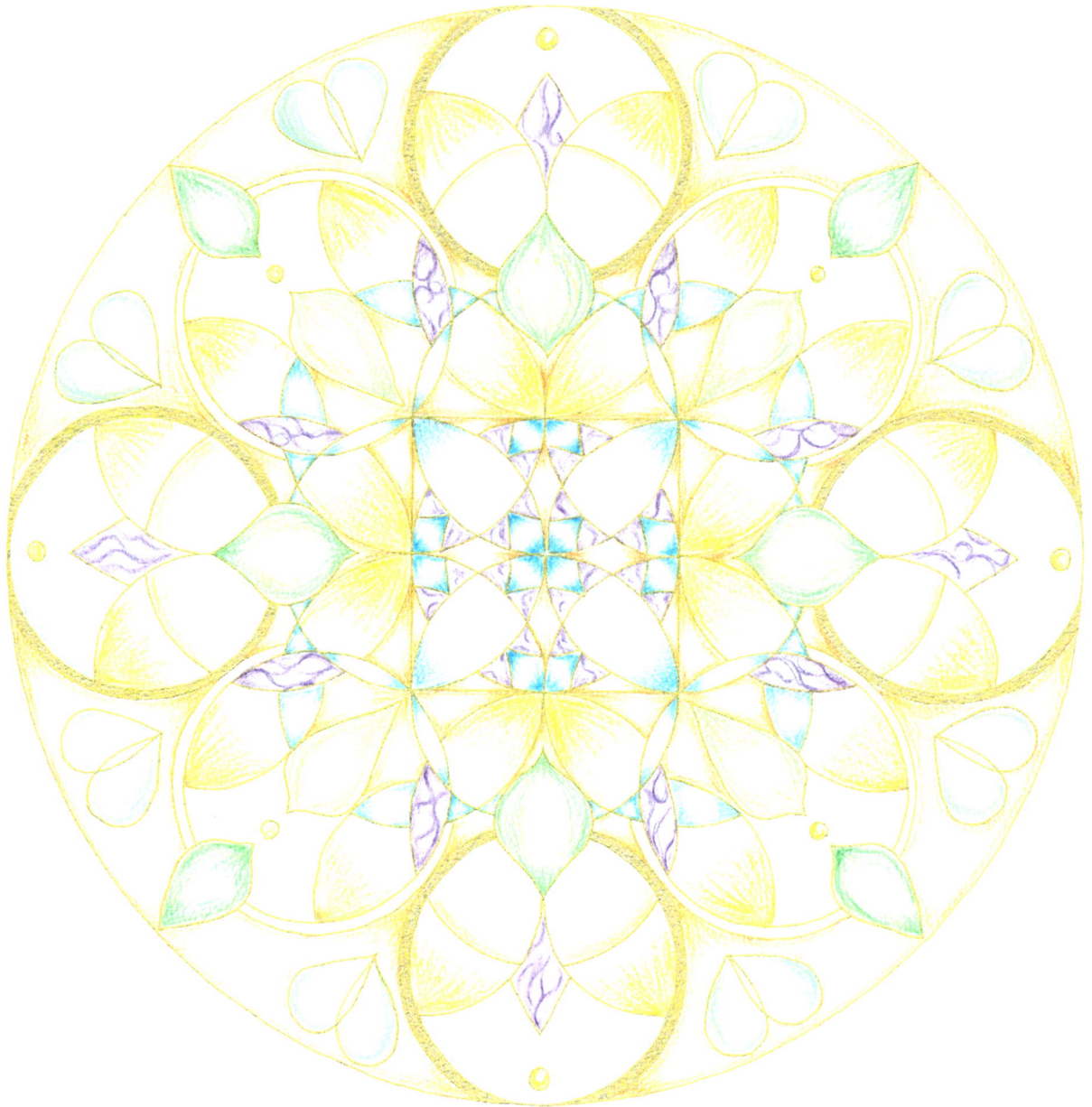

Mind Creates Reality

Do you realize that your visual looks, friends, job environment, health etc....are created by yourself? Your body cells are feeling the vibration from what you say, what you feel, what you think. Your cells are listening and you are creating your reality. If you feel unlucky, try speaking in a more positive way. If you make positivity your routine, your cell vibration will change and create a sparkling, beautiful life. What kind of situation are you in now? Do not forget, your mind creates your reality.

Bergamot

Bergamot connects you to your heart chakra. It adjusts your chi flow and it refreshes your body & mind. If your energy is not flowing well, you feel frustration and that life is a struggle. That makes you angry, jealous, nervous, and causes chaos within your spirit.
Bergamot will adjust your chi alignment and reset your body and mind with a kind but bright energy.

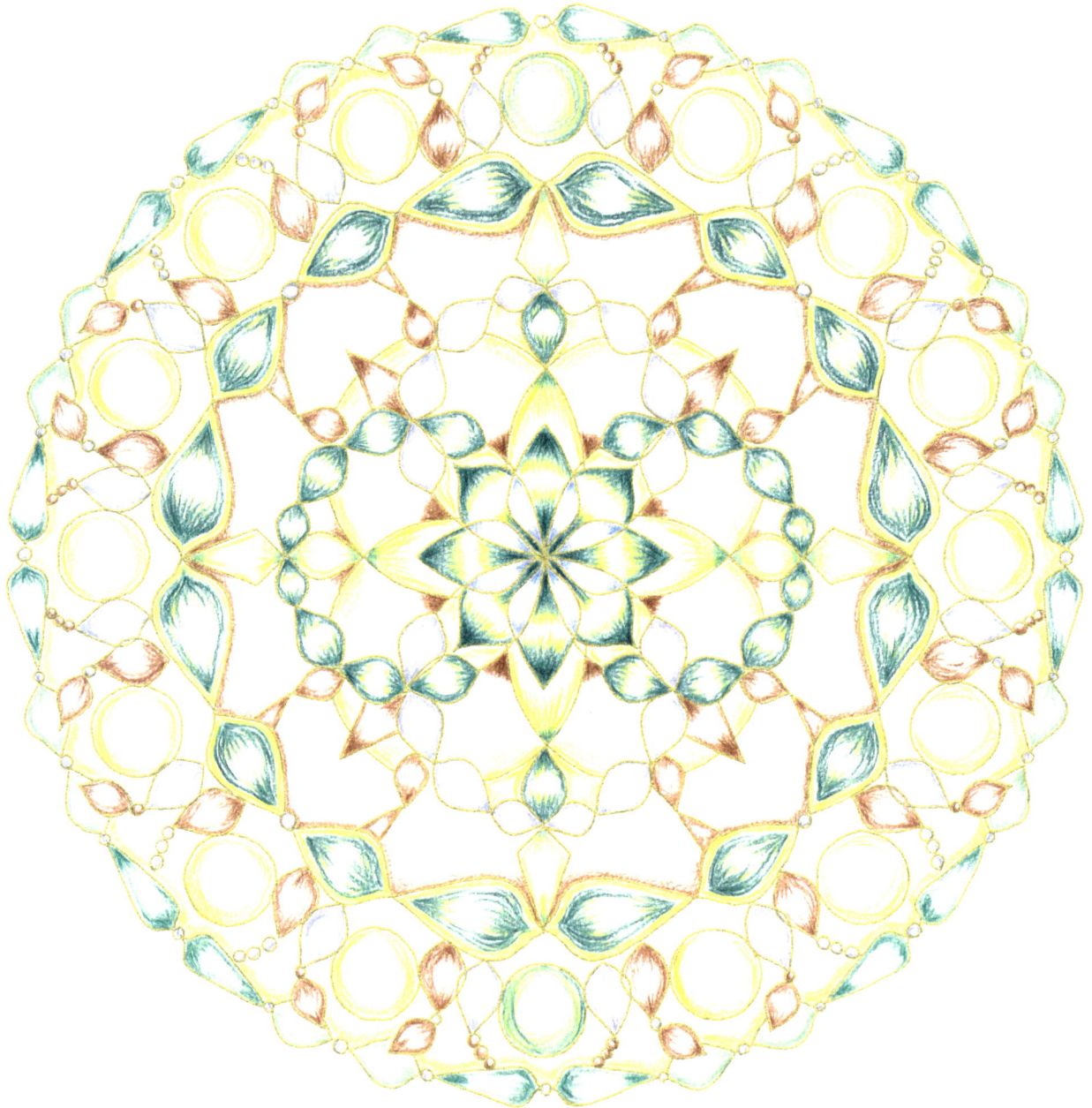

Big loss is hiding great luck!

When you get in big trouble, how does it make you feel? Most likely you feel upset, sad, afraid, angry, disappointed and you might lose yourself in the moment. However this is a great chance to change yourself and life. You will be able to see another way to go and maybe this new direction will bring you even more happiness. Sometimes you need empty your hands to receive good luck. You don't want to miss your Luck because your hands were full. So, think about it this way, there is great luck behind a big loss!

Caraway

Caraway is a symbol of purification. This sweet but spicy scent centers your energy and clears your digestive system both physically and spiritually. It may also greatly help you channel your higher self to get some advice and ideas about where you're supposed to go.

Charisma

Please realize you have great Charisma (light). Just like you see others have bright energy in their aura, you are also vibrating your own bright light. This is Truth. Do not ignore your light. If you find your light, then you will see the world is brighter. Your light is always inside of you with love. It does not waiver. It is without shame, without anger, without fear or self importance. It does not force. It just exists within you in silence.

Jasmine

Jasmine is a sweet but bright scent that gives you warmth and harmonic energy and you will begin to feel more confident.

Infinity

Your potential is infinite if you believe in yourself. Melissa will start vibrating your heart so that you can positively wield your spirit. This vibration will expand to the people around you. No one can set limits on you. Only you set the limits of your life.
We all have great and wonderful potential within us.

Melissa

Melissa relieves strong, stressful feelings such as fear, anger, anxiety and animosity. This fresh herb scent will guide you from narrow minded to open minded thoughts in a natural way. It protects you from the negative energy of others and from the environment as well. This is one of the keys to open and expand your Heart Chakra into infinity.

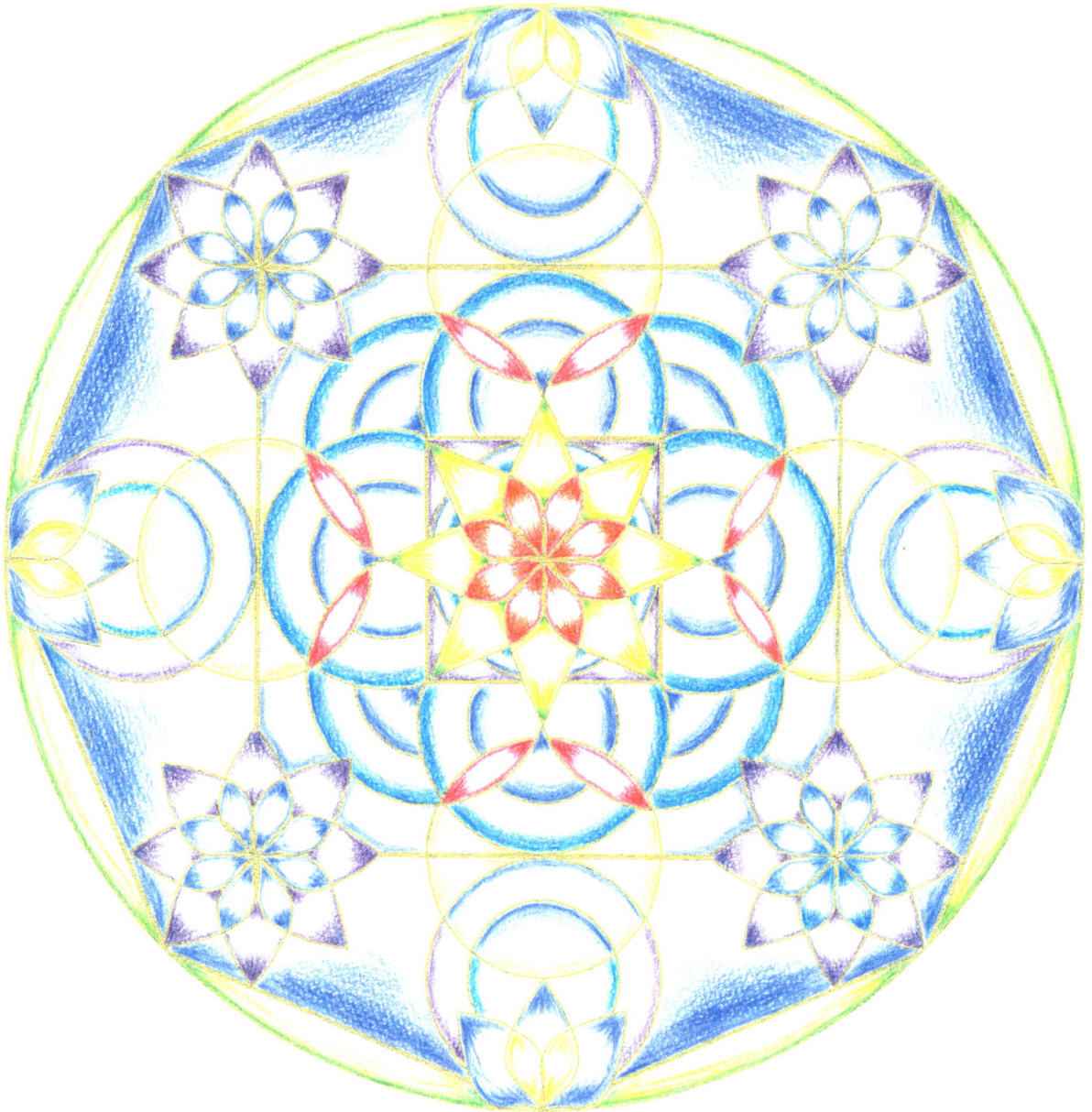

Real

Nobody can perfectly copy what you do. Even if somebody tries, it will not last long because it is not their truth, it is yours. They are lying to themselves. The real truth is strong and endures over time while imitations are limited. Real is real, imitation is imitation.

Frankincense

Frankincense is very popular in Europe to purify the energy at religious ceremonies. This purifies any vibrations of discord in your heart and helps your intuition.

Judging

People who criticize others do not define those they criticize. Rather, they end up defining themselves. If you really feel negative about something, meditate on it and develop how you want to live. Criticism is like a mirror into your own flaws and weaknesses.

Vetiver

Vetiver creates a balanced flow from outer to inner Chi. It grounds you. It guides you to focus on yourself and not others.

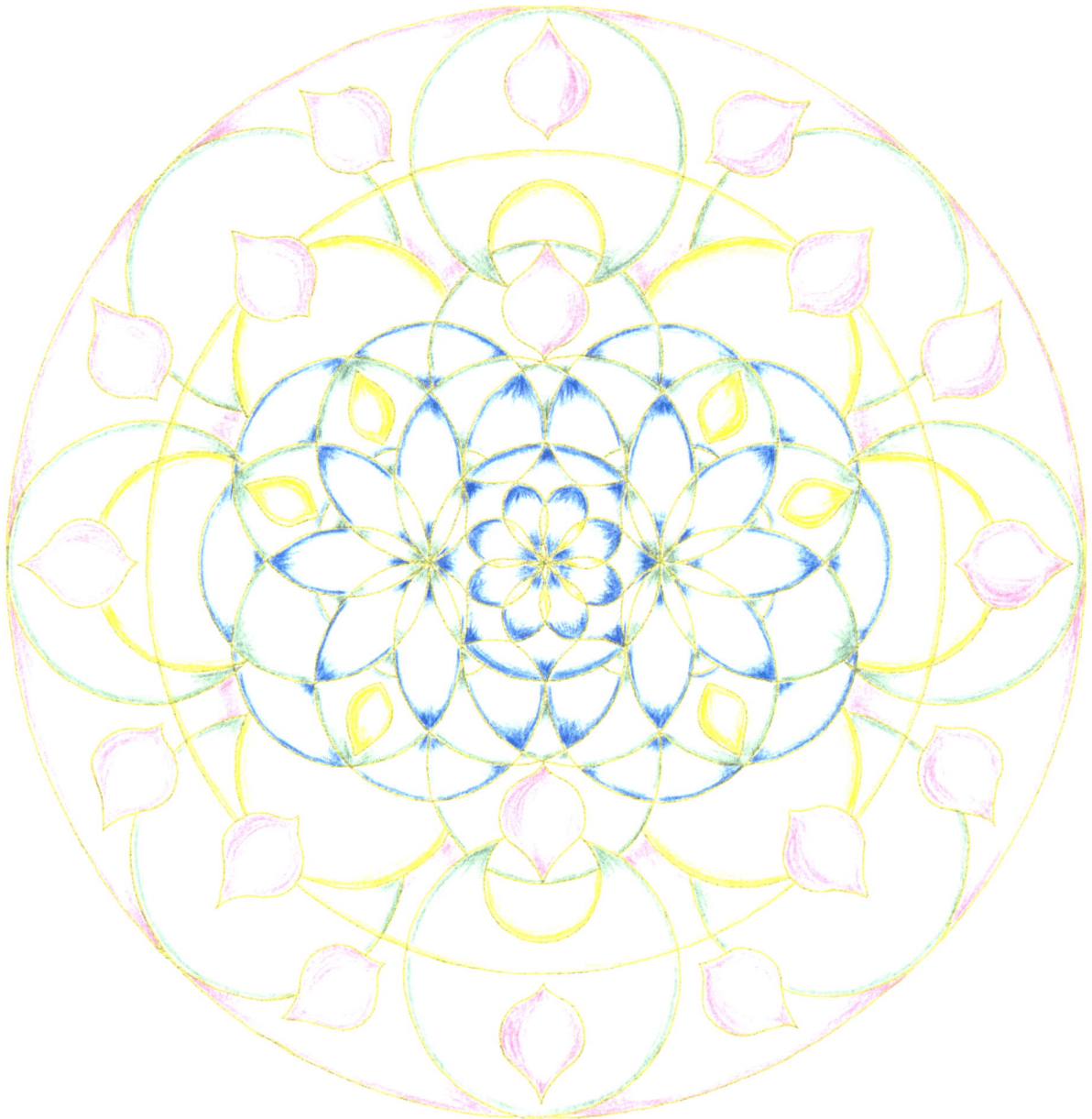

Truth

The truth is always there at the bottom of the water. However, when the wind blows and makes waves, this stirs things up and clouds the waters. Now you can't see what is in the water. If you see things through your emotions, it's like looking at cloudy water. You will lose sight of the right decision and your goal will slip even further away. The picture you see in the cloudy waters of your emotions is only the surface, not the truth. Don't focus only on this picture. Calm down your fear, anxiety and clear out your heart…the truth is under the water.

Geranium

Geranium creates a quiet and peaceful feeling. It will calm your turbulent, emotional waters to bring about clarity. It will not only help with fear and anxiety but also frustration and impatience. It will help center the spirit.

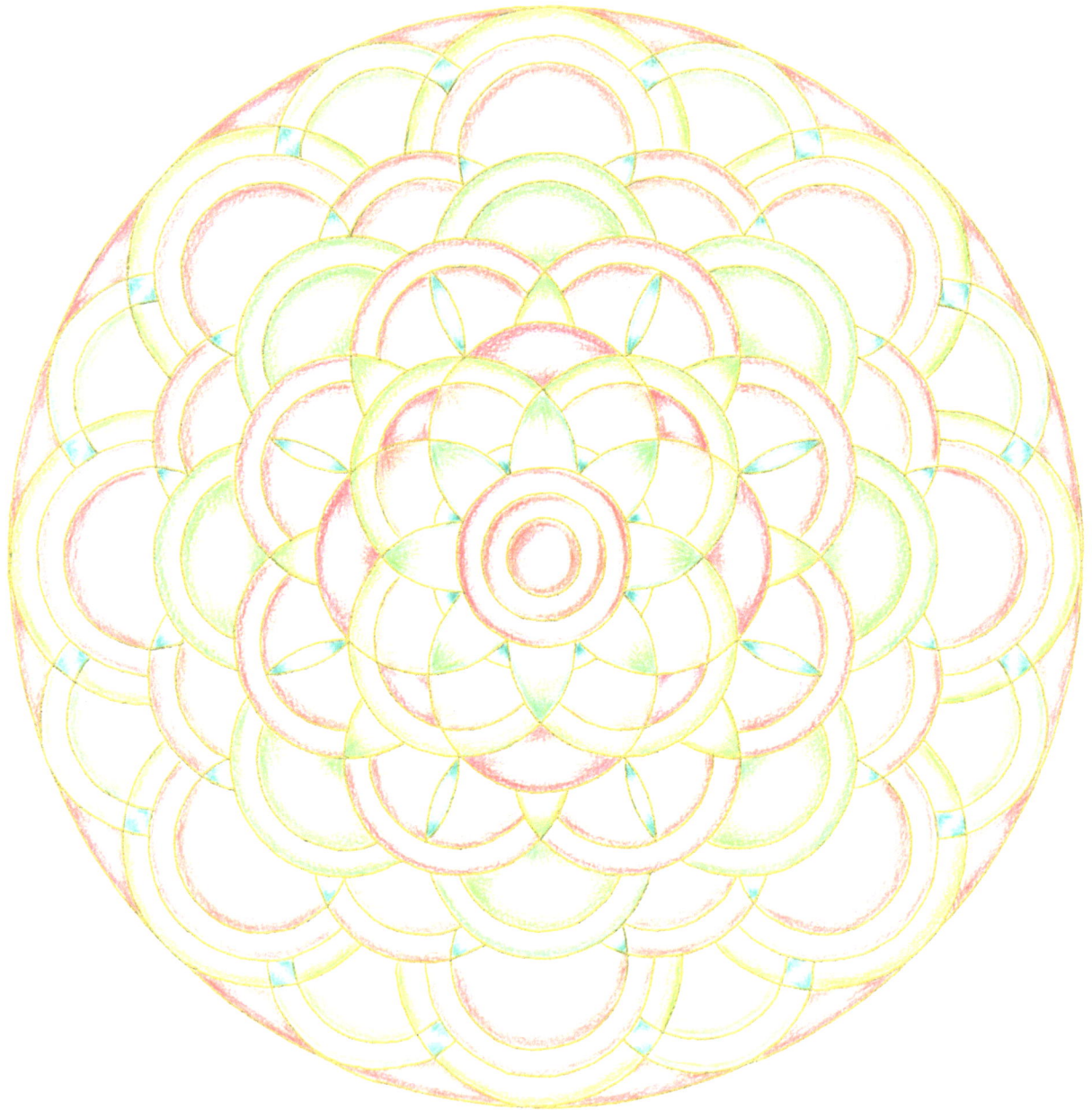

Appreciation

You probably know many people who appreciate their living environment and the people who helped them, even animals and plants, for enriching their lives. Perhaps you too give thanks for these things in your life. However, how many people appreciate there own body? The heart, liver, kidneys and all other organs are working hard to maintain our bodies so that we may live comfortably. The body cells are communicating with us through vibrations. Let's say "thank you" to our body cells. Each cell will respond and shine brightly giving us health and happy life.

Clary Sage

Clary Sage is a kind and warm oil that will bring warmth to your body, mind, heart, and aura. It will give you feelings of happiness and bring balance and abundance to your life.

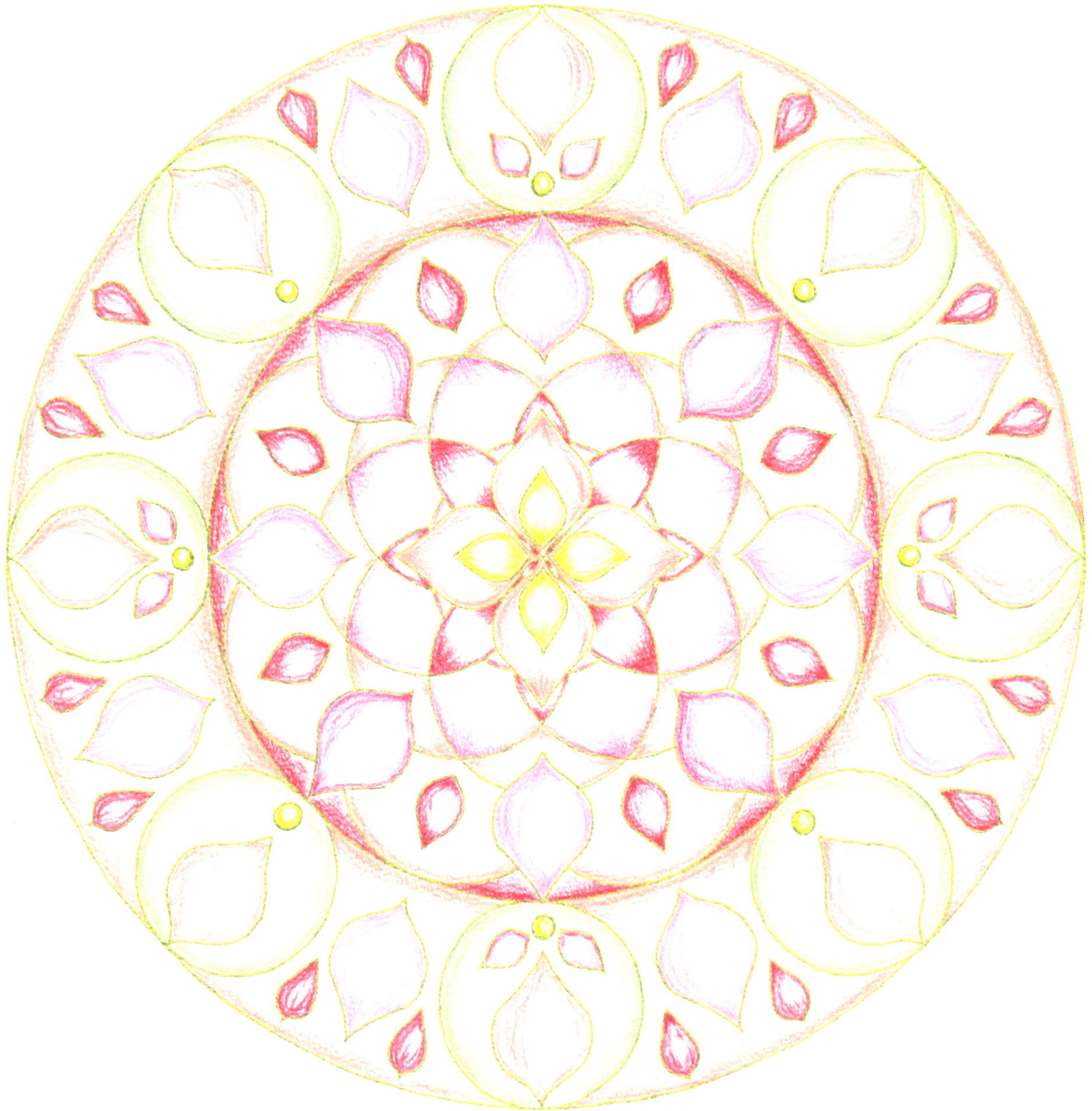

The secret medicine

The secret spice of medicine is "Love." Unexpected Love is the strongest and most powerful healing tool. It heals everything. So love yourself and love others.

Rose

The Rose is called The Queen of Flowers. This sweet scent deeply heals the dark side of your heart. It will also provide you with feelings of happiness and trust.

Attention

You don't have to speak loudly about how great you are. A truly great person is always humble and just smiles. If you speak loudly about yourself too much, that's just a cry for attention.

Cypress

Cypress oil will calm your heart's voice. It allows you to speak more objectively and calm down. It will help you accept what's happening around you.

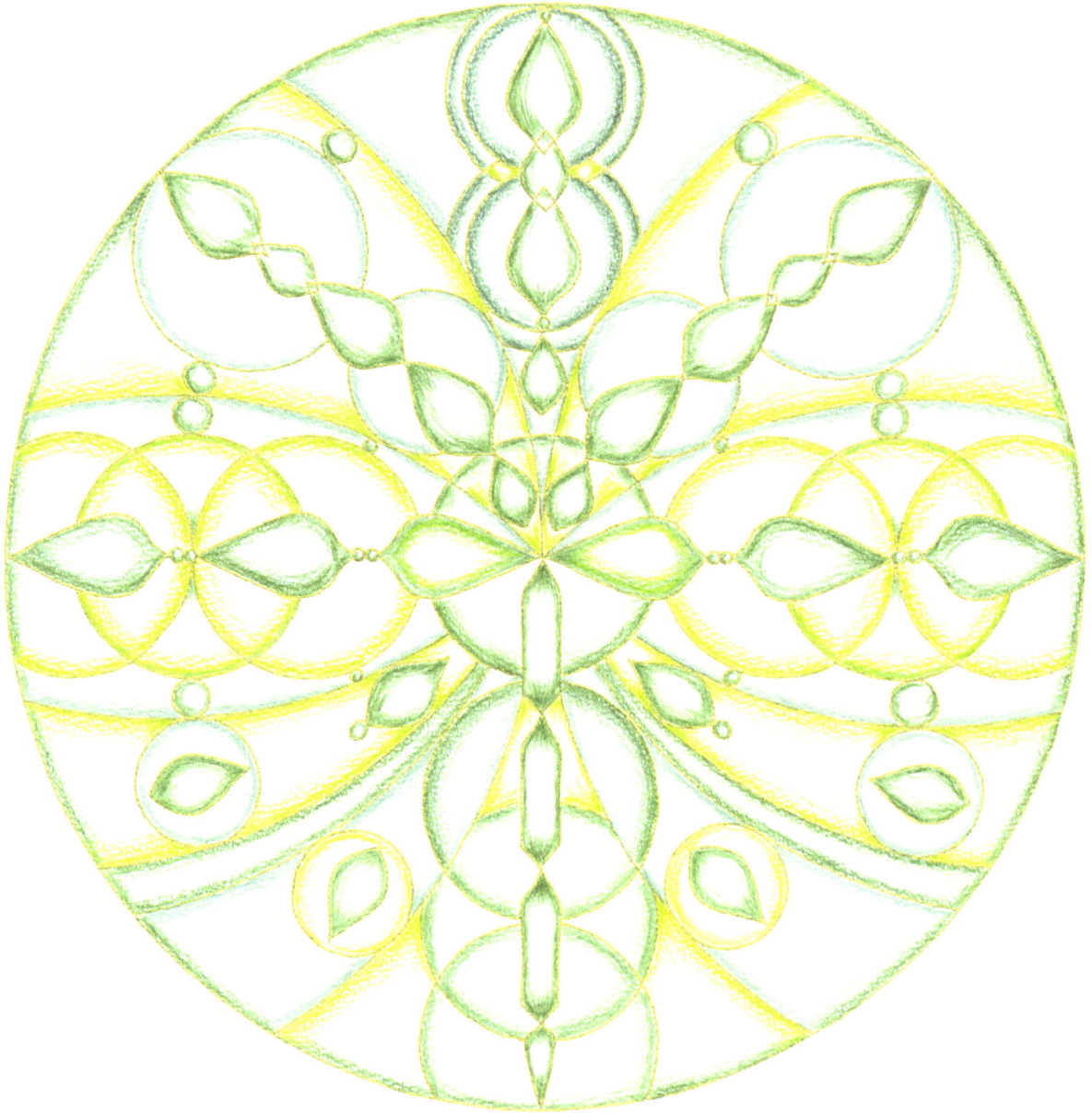

Expanding

If you share your wisdom (knowledge) from your heart without expecting anything in return, people will naturally follow you.
Don't be insecure and selfish, share it! Your energy will expand and people will feel it.
Then, you will notice people following you!

Verbena (Lemon Verbena)

Verbena is a fresh morning scent that releases the insecurities in your heart and guides you on a new road. This scent will teach you the joys of opening your heart and following a different path. It has both a refreshing and relaxing effect and will relieve all of your negative stress.

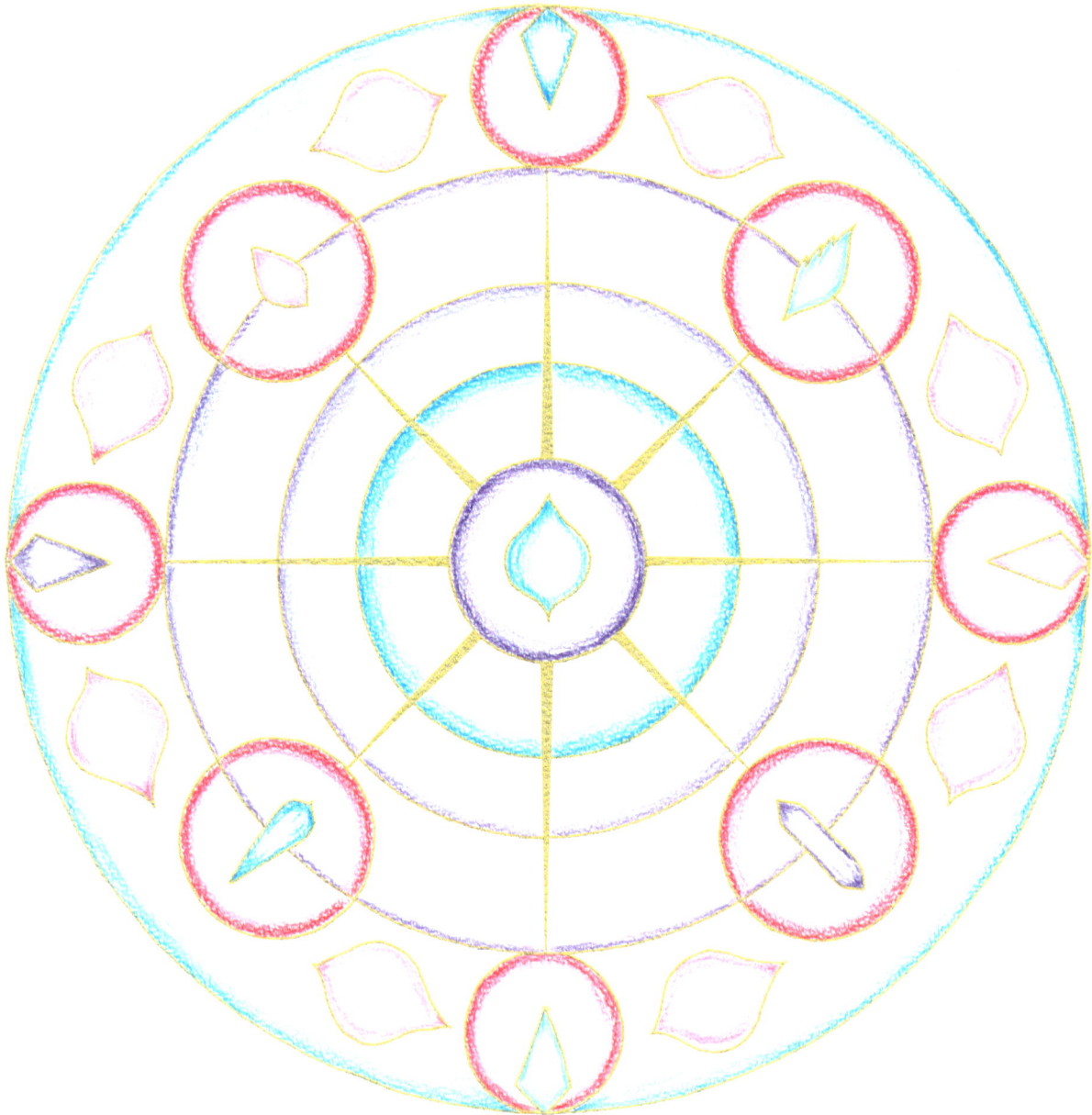

One step at the time

Deal with one step; once you've completed that, you can focus on the next step. If you do everything at once, you can't see what is going on. It is very important that you focus on things one at the time. It allows you to taste the fruits of your effort and keep your motivation to finish.

Rosemary

Rosemary is very popular for sharpening your brain. It clears all other thoughts from your mind and helps you concentrate on one thing.

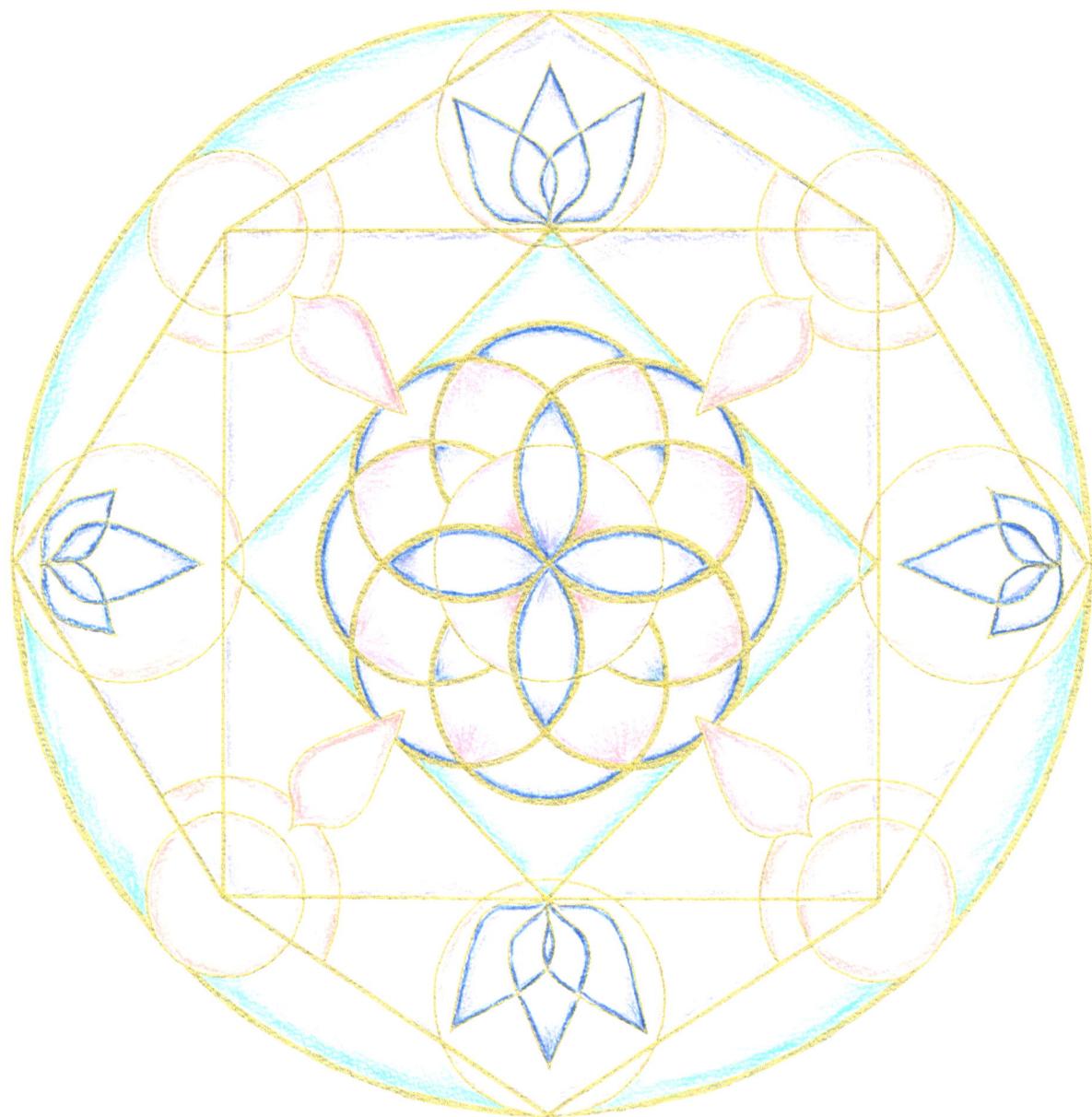

There is a time to share your knowledge

Persuasion is the ability to convince someone of something. Although, much of the time, our advice falls upon deaf ears. It is perhaps better to improve yourself and lead by example. If your self development shines, people will be curious about it and ask questions. This is the time to share your knowledge. It will fall on much more attentive and interested ears.

Hyssop

Hyssop is a spicy but fresh scent that will re-balance your emotions and guide you to be more logical and think clearly. It will support you to choose the best words for your presentation.

Consideration

People who are not considerate of others only think of themselves. It's a one way conversation. It is very important to sense and imagine other's situations and feelings before you take action.

Benzoin

Benzoin is a sweet vanilla-like scent that will give you a warm, kind and heartfelt feeling.

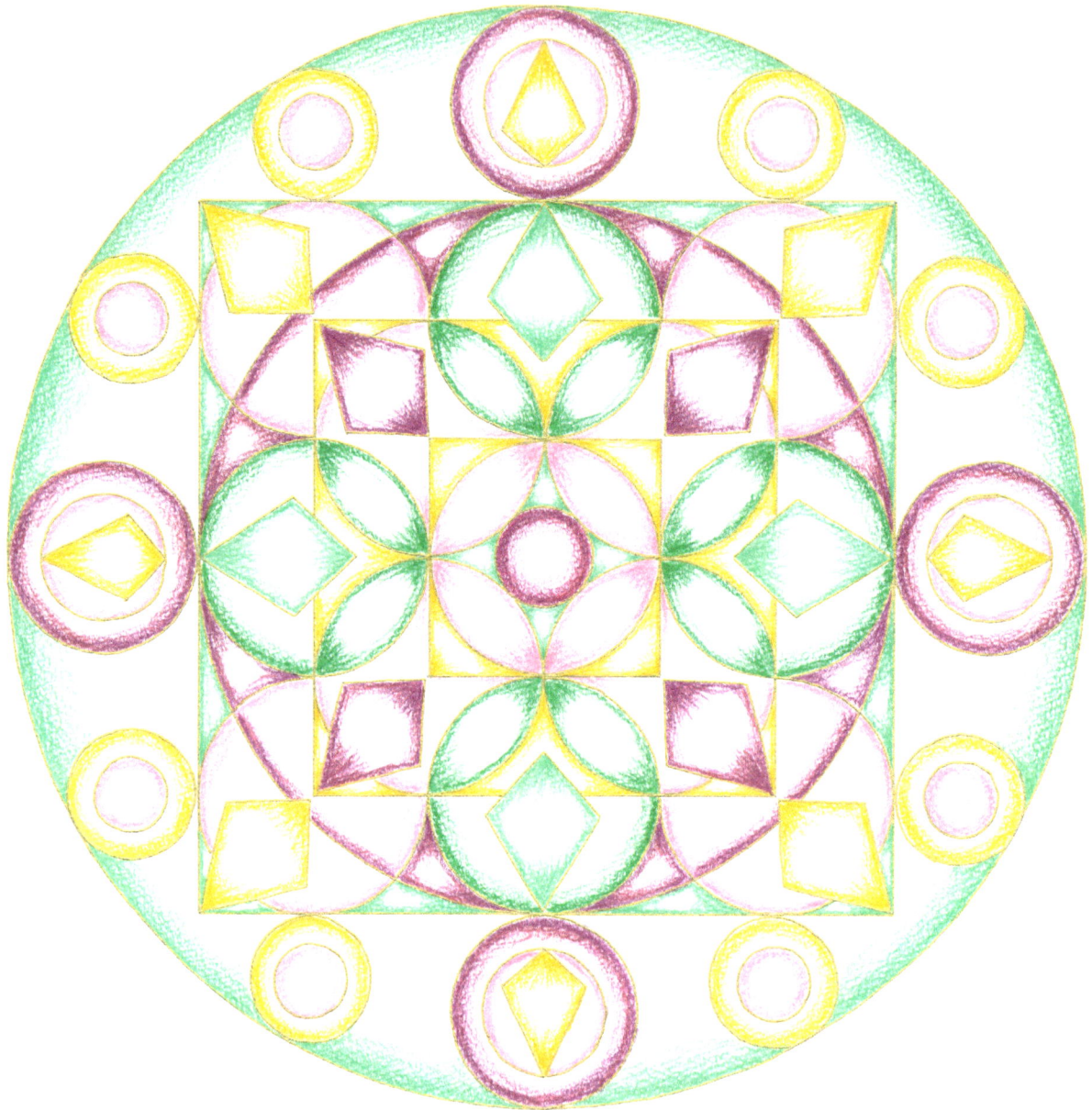

Fastest way to reach your goal

If you skip the foundation, ignore the steps in the process and jump ahead, you will see that you have to go back to the beginning later. And it will take more time and more effort than you expect. There are no short cuts in life. We need to faithfully and humbly work through the process. Realize that this is the fastest way to reach your goal!

Basil

Basil is a fresh, herbal scent that calms down our rushed feelings and sharpens the brain to focus on the goal. This will cleanse all your toxic thoughts and pull you up to a higher dimension.

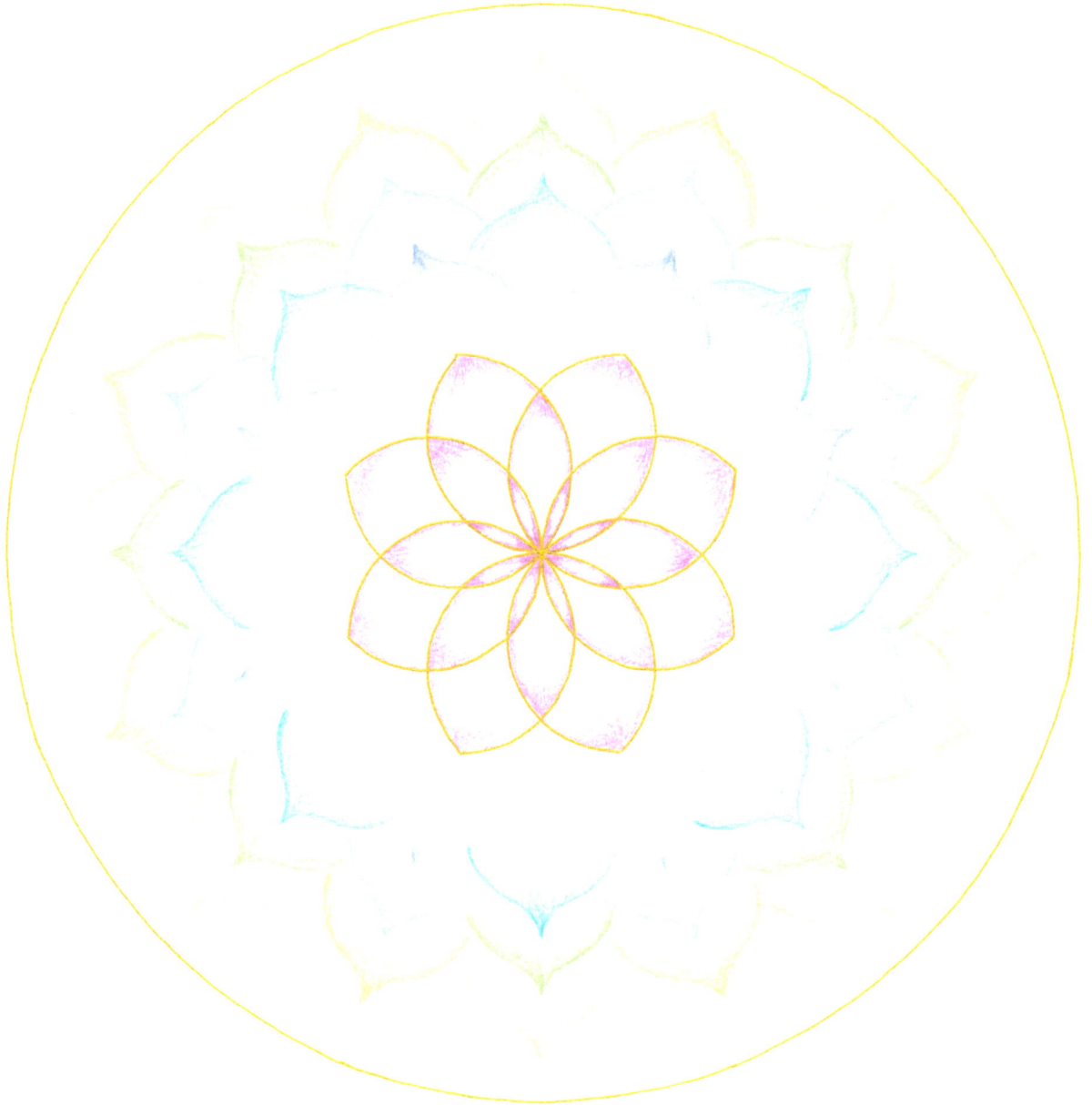

Compassion

Compassion is not giving everything you have to others and expending all of your energy. Compassion is the ability to share your wisdom with others for their regeneration and independence. Only a little bit of your energy is needed to truly help others. Share your inner wisdom in a way that is appropriate given their age, personality, and balance of energy so that you can help them understand how to further their journey. (For example: you would explain things differently to a child compared to an adult.)

White Lotus

White Lotus is a rainbow vibration of high dimension. A white light connects us from heaven to earth. It gives us advice to choose the right words for others in any situation.

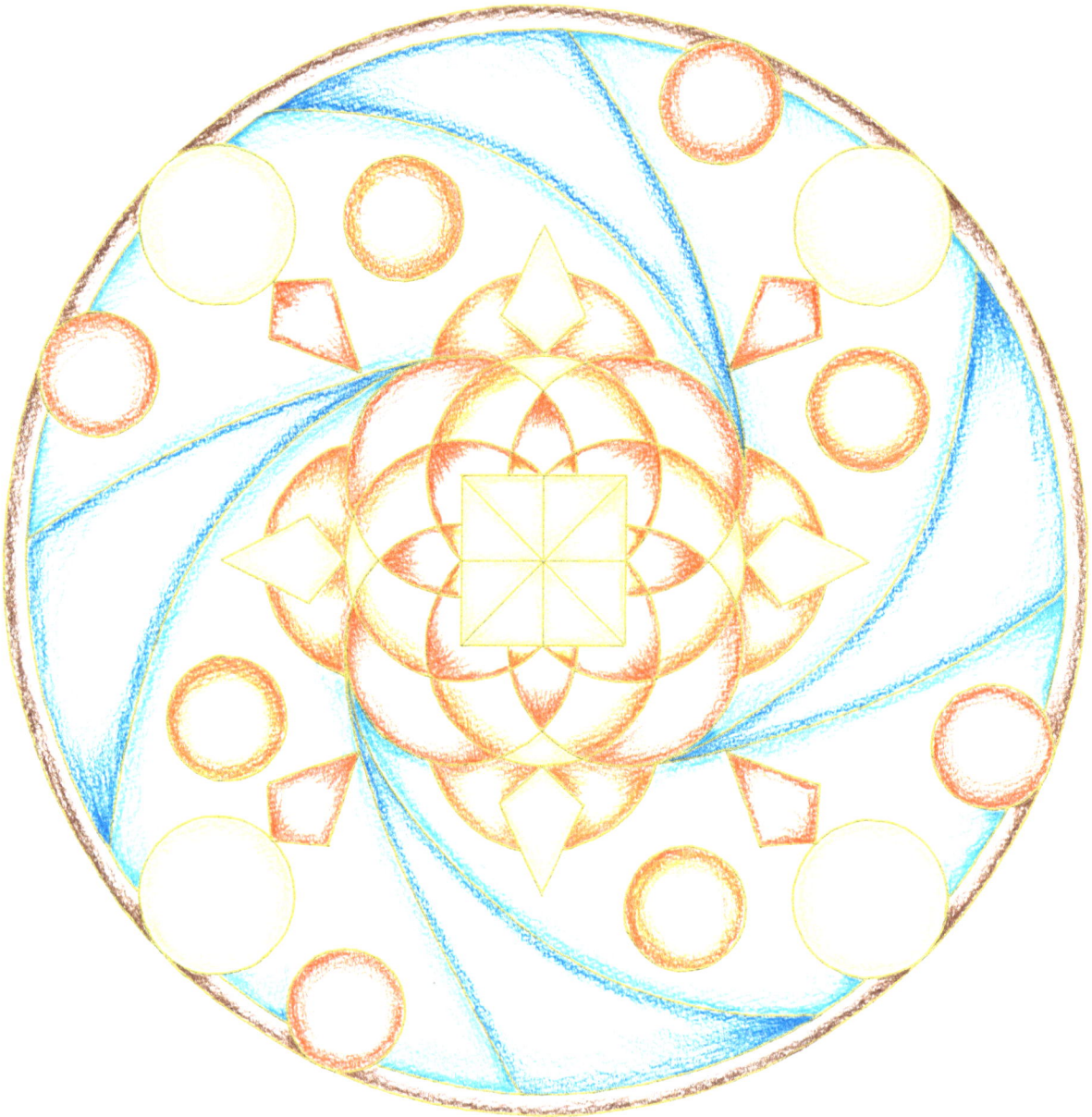

Experience

Experience will become self confidence. At some point, everyone was a beginner. If you continue to pursue your interest, perhaps one day it will be your specialty. Is there something that you are putting off because you think it is difficult? Instead of avoiding it, do it as soon as possible. You can minimize your negative feelings and save time. The more you get used to this thing then you will develop another skill to make you feel confident! You will see that your world will be more relaxed and fun.

Petitgrain

Petitgrain is from an orange tree with a soft and fresh scent which will help you calm down and sharpen your brain to make better decisions. It will support you to take action!

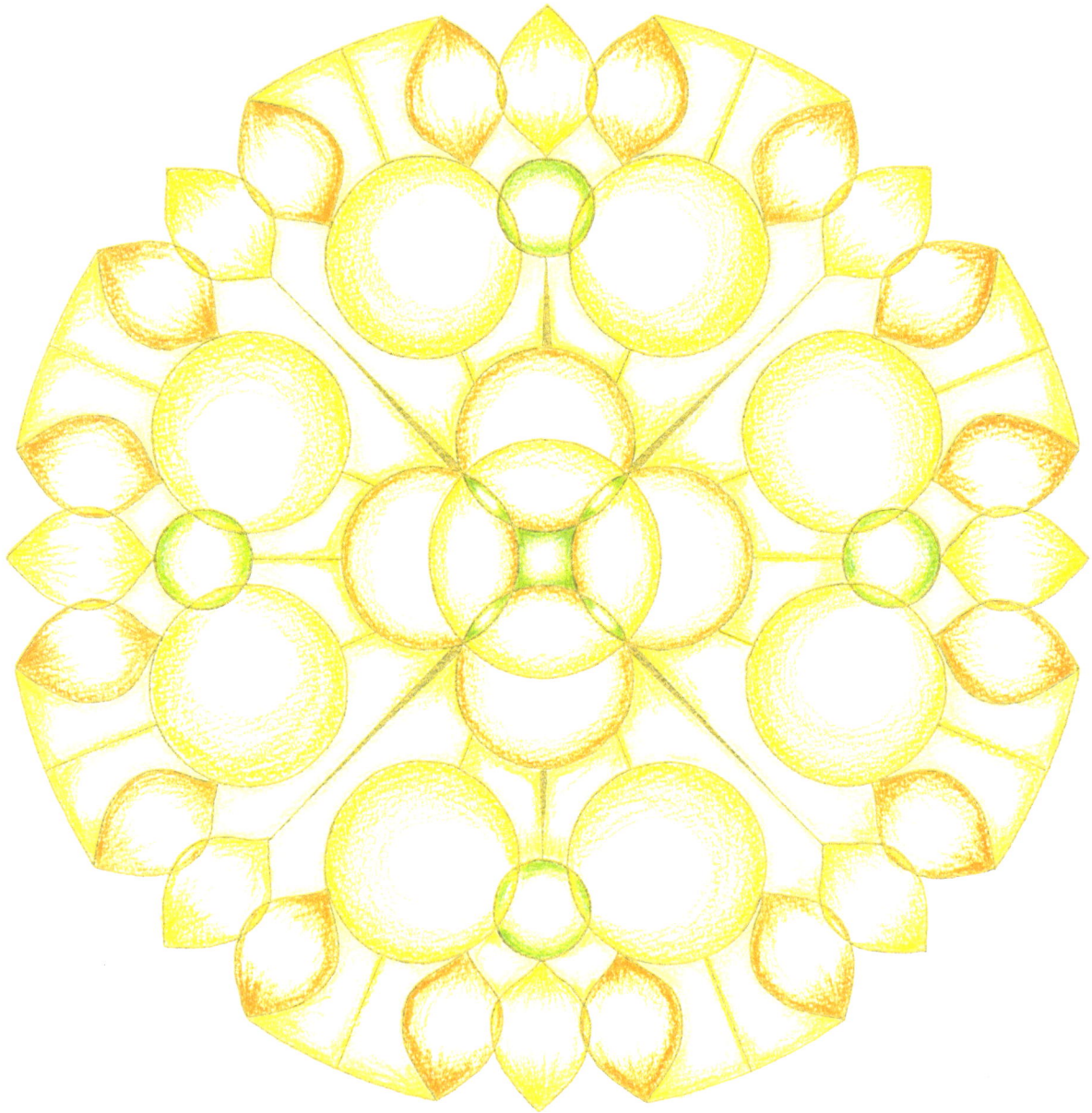

We are all special

We all may look similar but we are all special. We are unique and have our own individual bright light. So stop fighting to be a best of the world. Realize that there is no need to compete and prove that you are better than others because we are already special and unique. Just like a tulip grows straight towards the sky from a ball without doubt, you can grow your own flower in the same way. Tulips have different sizes and colors but they don't fight each other, because they know they are all special, beautiful, worth and proud to be a tulip.

Lemongrass

Lemongrass scent releases frustration and has been loved by India for a long time. This scent not only calms you down but also puts the right energy in your heart and guides you to the right energy flow. You will feel peace and confidence about yourself.

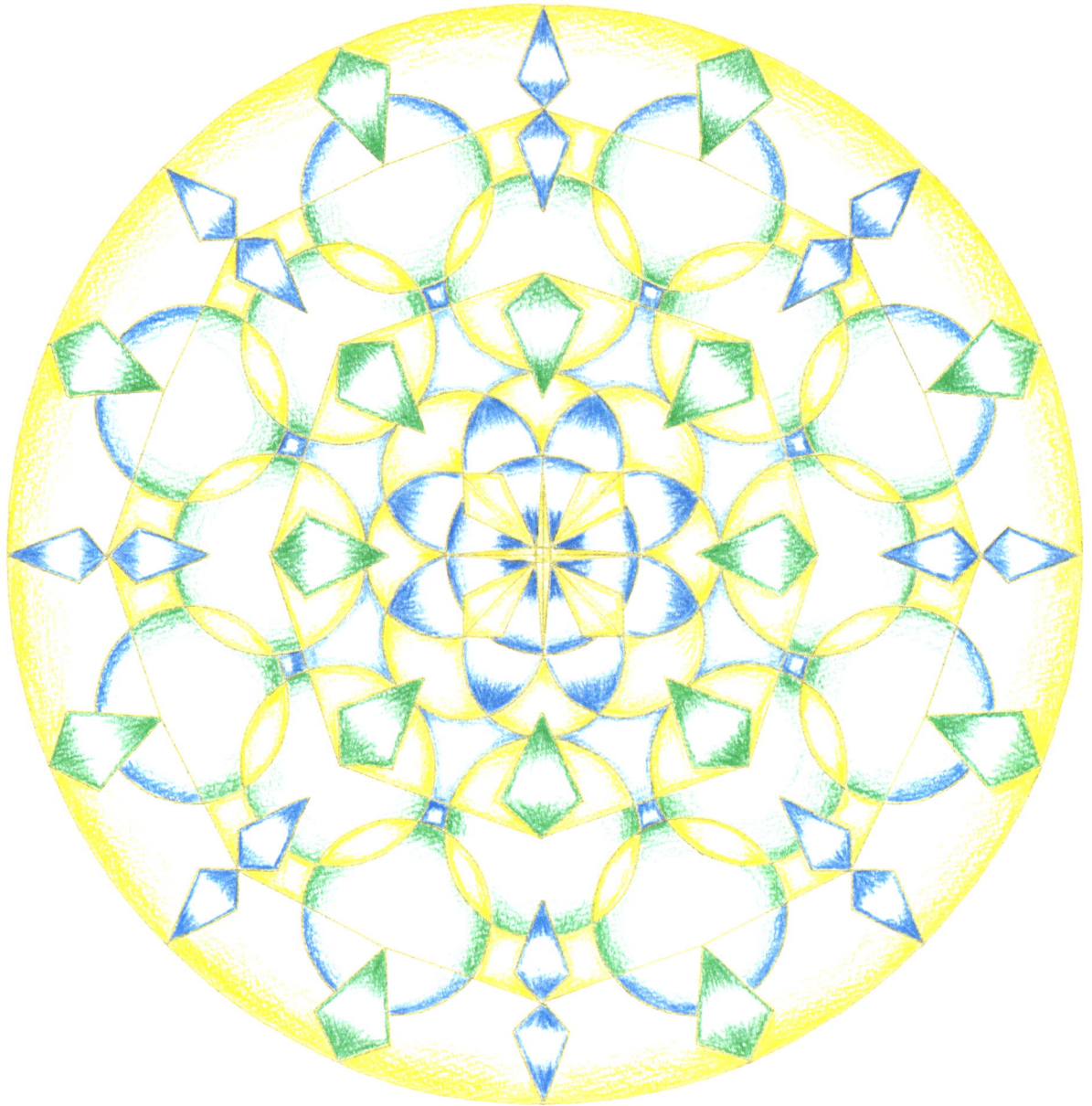

Others are a mirror of you

You have a great chance to develop yourself by observing others. If you feel annoyed by other people's negative attitude, that means you also have a part of you that is like them. If you complain about gossip, then you become just like them. Words have spirit and vibrations which are alive, but you don't realize that these negative thoughts circle back to choke yourself. Think about your life like a magnet. Negative thoughts draw negative people to you. Positive thoughts will draw positive people to you. So if you experience a negative situation, look inward and develop yourself! If you are truly in a good state of being, you are supposed to have good and supportive people around you! This is a great opportunity to change your life!

Chamomile

Chamomile represents both the Sun and the Moon. It affects your solar plexus (behind the stomach) and balances the 3rd & 4th chakras to center your energy. It makes you calm down and also gives you good energy. You discover what you want for your life and it will help you make it happen.

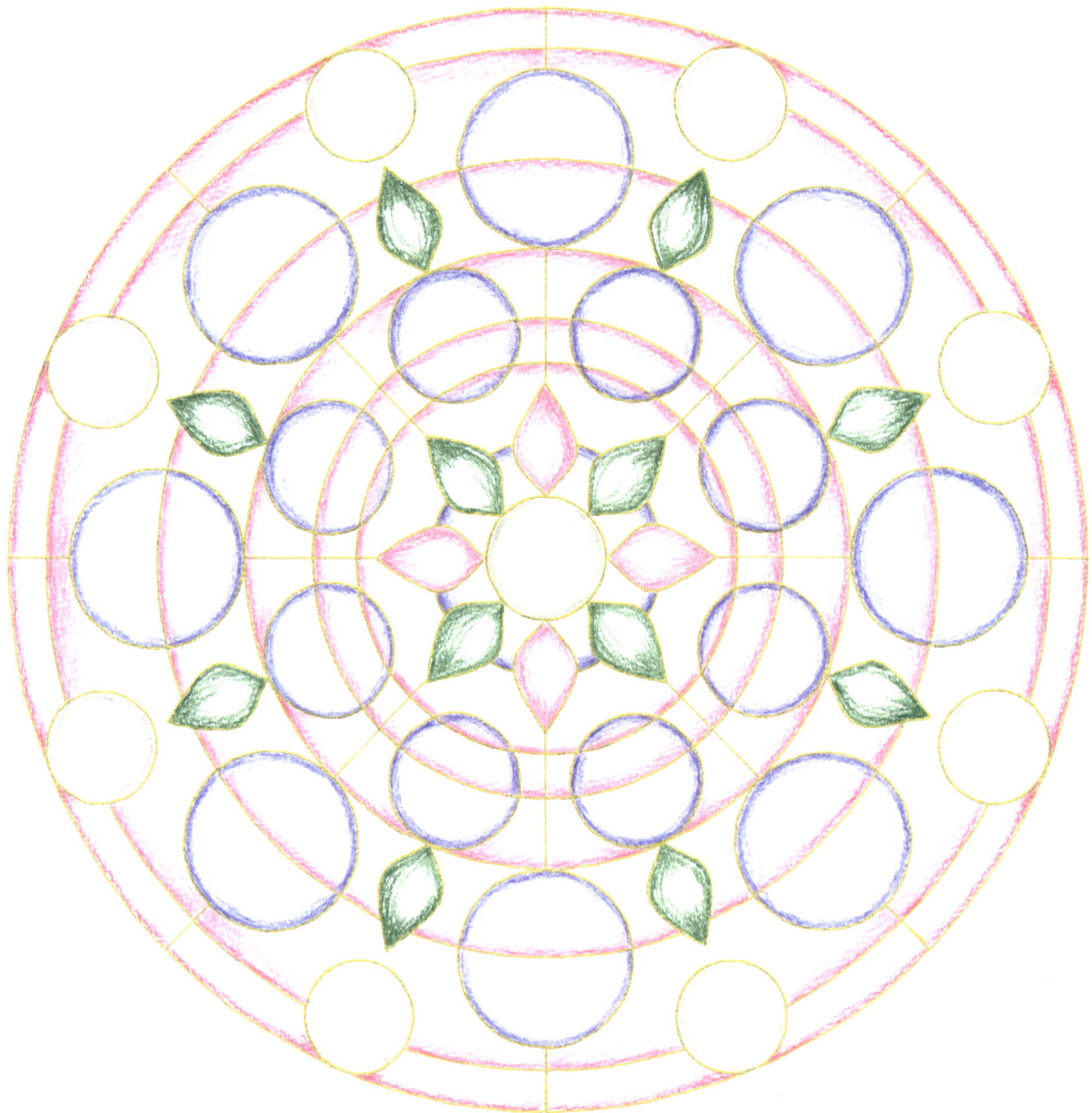

The round communications

The shape of pyramid communication revolves around ego and is based on using power.
The shape of round communication is harmonious and is based on respect. If everybody feels comfortable and happy, it will build confidence and cooperation with each other. This increases energy and projects strong vibrations. You will see the world like a water drop expanding infinitely. Everybody is a leader and everybody is a follower. You feel fulfilled and realize that you have created a great thing!

Spikenard

Spikenard will shift your weak and unpleasant feelings into love. It helps you base your communications on trust and peace. Spikenard is charging energy for your heart and soul and guides you to harmony.

Break time

If your gas tank is empty, it is time to take a rest. You have been running non-stop for a long time. Your body, mind and spirit gets confused and you can start to get sick. Slow down and give them rest. If you also feel frustration, just put your feelings aside. Maybe it is not the time to harvest. Sometimes you need to be alone and detoxify, charging your energy to move forward. Don't worry, slowness brings clarity, clarity brings purpose and purpose speeds things up! Do not rush, take your time to build a good foundation and prepare for the harvest!

Marjoram

Marjoram relaxes your tense energy and gathers all of your Chi to your center. This scent of mother earth heals rushed feelings with warmth. It can also give you great quality sleep!

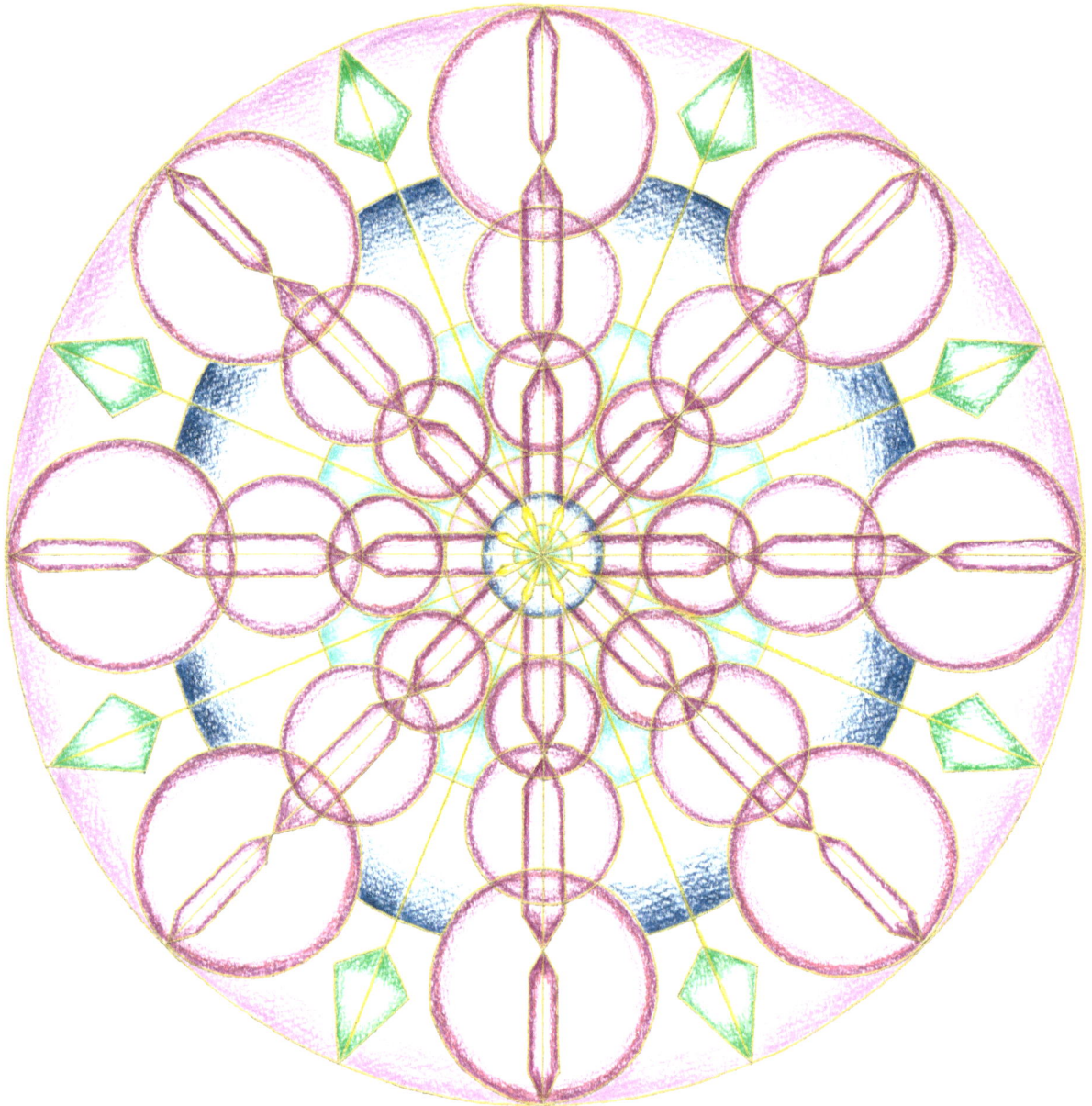

Non Physical Vibration

You have been growing your 1st, 2nd and 3rd chakras. You have a lot of experiences that you can incorporate into your life. You are very grounded and you have good trust from others. However, you are too much in the physical world and cannot see the whole truth. You know that there is more to this world than just the physical vibrations, but you can't see it. You have a good foundation, but now it is time to study the 5th, 6th and 7th spiritual (non-physical) chakras to connect you to the universe. Put the spice in your soul and feel your heart expanding. This makes you feel open and invites a wider world into your life!

Lavender

Lavender not only opens and balances your physical body but also your aura. It helps you with conflict, contradiction and dilemmas. You will feel abundance in your heart while incorporating the truth.

Physical Vibration

Your 6th and 7th chakra is very open and strong. Like a baby's pure energy, it makes you feel good, always connecting to your higher self. You have intuition and charisma and it gives you great talent. However, if you look at your life on the physical plane, you probably have friction in communicating with others and you are also strongly influenced by your surroundings.

The 1st, 2nd, and 3rd chakras will help you become more down to earth and grounded.

Now, it is the time to learn and make these chakras stronger! It is a wake up call!

Try to appreciate your families and ancestors (even though you did not know or grow up with them.) You don't have to go to see them, just take a moment in your heart to project your appreciation of them. This act will strengthen these chakras.

Try to do Yoga, Tai Chi, or Qi Gong, for feeding energy to your chakras. This will expand and refresh your vision. You feel a rise in your happiness!

Sandal Wood

Sandalwood has been very popular for religion and meditation since ancient time. It makes you very grounded but still allows a spiritual gathering of all energy to your center. It unifies your calmness and energy to guide you to Zen.

Forest (your community and identity)

Sometimes you need to explore. If you are brave enough to step out into the world, you will know what kind of forest you have been living in. You will see how big your forest is, what its shape is like, what kind of trees are around you and what kind of tree are you?

To study your forest from the outside looking in, you will gain a better sense of your identity. You start to become proud of where you are from, the culture you have, and yourself! You will feel this more heart-fully and the world will be brighter and sparkle for you.

Fennel

Fennel is a floral and spicy scent that increases energy and makes your heart brave. It releases your tension from an overactive mind. It will support you to step out!

Forgiveness

If you see a person who is totally different and it seems like you have nothing in common, how do you react to this person? You probably exclude them from your life or they cause you to have negative thoughts or prejudice. However, instead of taking it negatively, why don't we open our hearts to them? Don't take anything personally, just let it go. Then, your heart will be expanding and the universe will guide you to oneness (fusion). You and others are given salvation by the universe and blessed by the light (enlightenment). So instead of cutting them out of your life, acknowledge and appreciate that there are many different people, so that you move towards the enlightenment. If you understand that they also bring value and have a place in this world, you can feel your heart will become more peaceful and appreciative.

Rosewood

Rosewood is a sweet and woody mysterious scent that makes you warm and melts a hardened heart. It wakes your female side up to embrace tolerance.

Epilogue

This book based on the Japanese Culture that I learned since I was little. It was very exciting when I truly understood what those traditions meant. I my soul felt free and started to see the world in a totally different light.

So....I made this book humbly to share with you.

Before we were born, we chose the roadmap of our Karma and we laid it out before us to discover. These subjects are like the home work of our lives to live on the Earth.

The universe is testing us to see how much we can enjoy and release our ego to explore these ideas.

I hope this book inspires and enlightens you, guiding you to freedom…

Special Thank you

Thanks to all my families, friends and teachers who gave me awareness and knowledge.

A special thank you to Mandala Artist "Ruan" for visualizing my inspirations into art.

Thank you to my husband Bruce Wee for helping in the process of making this book and checking my English.

Thank you for my dear friend Brooke Bingaman for the final touch up of the all massage parts and some others. I especially want to thank her for knowledge of the language of spirituality to help out in correcting each paragraph.

 # Ruan

Ruan is originally from Japan and has been a clown artist for many years, performing on the stage and at many events. Her talented art sense can be found not only in her performance but also through her drawings.

She found inspiration in drawing Mandalas with color pencils in 2011.

Her Mandala Art started to show her talent immediately, and her truly pure Zen energy began to flow out into the public amazingly.

Lately, she is doing a Healing Mandala Art workshop with colored pencils and message sessions. I commissioned her to draw these Mandalas to help visualize the special energy that comes from nature and these oils.

English- weesenseproect@yahoo.co.jp
Japanese- ruan.y.s.p@aol.jp
          http://ameblo.jp/ruan-work/

About the Author

Yoko Y. Wee

Yoko Wee is originally from Japan. She grew up in the beautiful seasons and historical culture found there. She spent a lot of time in nature and playing around in the Shinto Shrines where she grew up. Both grand parents gifted all their wisdom to this grand child.

She was lucky to be born into a unique family of Medical Doctors and School Teachers. Even her father was a pharmacist of both western and eastern medicine. She feels that the environment is a necessity to become an Aromatherapist and a Healing Guide. She has been instructing and healing since 1998. (In 2006, she opened an Aromatherapy school for Japanese in Honolulu.)

She is also talented as being a jazz, modern, and Argentine Tango dancer for many years. It gave her good training in how to "feel" with the music and harmonize with the body and mind. It gave her huge physical and spiritual development.

After she married, she moved to the beautiful Yang energy island of Hawai'i in 2003. This island has been giving her the opportunity to learn and open up her spiritual side.

Now, she is embodying both the Yin (Japan) and Yang (Hawai'i) energy, she felt it was her destiny to share this with others. She started to open Aromatherapy workshops in English and energy work sessions to dancers for their enrichment.

ありがとう

葉子

YokoWee.com

Credentials

*Seiyo Kunko Aromatherapy school certified Herb and Aroma coordinator
*Professional Aromatherapist member of the National Association for Holistic Aromatherapy
*5th generation of Usui shiki Reiki Healing
*2nd generation of Quantum Reiki Healing

*2nd degree license of kindergarten Education (Japan)
*2nd degree license of Elementary Education (Japan)
*NPO Japan Food educational Program Association Authorized -Food Educational Program instructor Primary
*Mental Health counselor (certified by Japan association)

Gifted to all of you...

Healing Mandala Art

"Songs from the Earth"

Note...

www.ingramcontent.com/pod-product-compliance
Lightning Source LLC
Chambersburg PA
CBHW061353090426
42739CB00002B/18